OXFORD BOOKWORMS LIBRARY

Factfiles

Stephen Hawking

ALEX RAYNHAM

Stage 2 (700 headwords)

Series Editor: Rachel Bladon
Founder Factfiles Editor: Christine Lindop

OXFORD
UNIVERSITY PRESS

Great Clarendon Street, Oxford, OX2 6DP, United Kingdom

Oxford University Press is a department of the University of Oxford.
It furthers the University's objective of excellence in research, scholarship,
and education by publishing worldwide. Oxford is a registered trade
mark of Oxford University Press in the UK and in certain other countries

ISBN: 978 0 19 402402 0

A complete recording of this Bookworms edition of *Stephen Hawking* is available.

Printed in China

Word count (main text): 6,425

For more information on the Oxford Bookworms Library,
visit www.oup.com/elt/gradedreaders

ACKNOWLEDGEMENTS

Cover images: Getty Images (Stephen Hawking/Ulrich Baumgarten); Shutterstock (black hole/REDPIXEL.PL).

The publisher would like to thank the following for their permission to reproduce photographs: Alamy pp.5 (University
College Oxford/Paul Weston), 30 (CBE medal/Mike Greenslade), 36 (*The Theory of Everything*); Gillman & Soame
pp.6 (Stephen Hawking as a rowing cox, 1961), 7 (Stephen Hawking graduating from Oxford, 1962); Getty
Images pp.3 (Galileo Galilei using a telescope, circa 1620/Hulton Archive/Stringer), 12 (Fred Hoyle at the
Institute of Astronomy in England, December 1967/Hulton-Deutsch Collection/Corbis), 16 (Albert Einstein in
Philadelphia, 1936/Popperfoto), 17 (The 4-D Space-Time Continuum Is Distorted In The Vicinity Of Any Mass/
Encyclopaedia Brittanica/Universal Images Group), 22 (Stephen Hawking on October 10, 1979 in Princeton,
New Jersey/Santi Visalli), 23 (Sir Isaac Newton/Hulton Fine Art Collection), 24 (Stephen Hawking inside
a lecture hall with math equations on blackboard behind him/Terry Smith/The LIFE Images Collection),
27 (Computer and speech synthesiser housing, 1999/Science & Society Picture Library), 27 (Stephen Hawking,
1989/Jean-Regis Roustan/Roger Viollet), 29 (Stephen Hawking, delivers a lecture entitled 'The Origin of the
Universe' at the Great Hall of the People June 19, 2006 in Beijing, China/China Photos/Stringer), 29 (Stephen
Hawking attends the lecture 'Universe' in Muizenberg at the African Institute for Mathematical Sciences May
11, 2008 in Cape Town, South Africa/Michelly Rall), 33 (Stephen Hawking appearing on *The Big Bang Theory*/
Sonja Flemming/CBS), 33 (US President Barack Obama presents the Presidential Medal of Freedom to Stephen
Hawking during a ceremony in the East Room at the White House on August 12, 2009/Jewel Samad/AFP),
35 (Stephen Hawking appears during the opening ceremony of the London 2012 Paralympic Games at the
Olympic Park in east London on August 29, 2012/Glyn Kirk/AFP), 39 (Stephen Hawking with his first wife Jane
Hawking, circa 1990/David Montgomery), 42 (Milky Way galaxy/Mark Garlick), 45 (Stephen Hawking attends
the gala screening of 'Hawking' on the opening night of the Cambridge Film Festival held at Emmanuel
College on September 19, 2013 in Cambridge, Cambridgeshire/Karwai Tang), 50 (Charles Babbage/Time Life Pictures/Mansell), 50 (Paul Dirac/Bettmann), 51 (A Caucasian
scientist working with a large telescope/iStock), 62 (Galileo Galilei by Francesco Boschi (1619–1675)/Fine Art
Images/Heritage Images); Professor Stephen Hawking p.4 (young Stephen Hawking/Mary Hawking); Herts
Advertiser p.5 (Stephen Hawking at St Albans School); Penguin Random House pp.31 (*A Brief History of Time*),
32 (*My Brief History*), 32 (*George's Cosmic Treasure Hunt* by Lucy & Stephen Hawking); Rex Shutterstock pp.iv
(Stephen Hawking/Errol Morris/Triton/Kobal), 34 (Stephen Hawking at Children's Hospital in Boston/Julia
Malakie/AP), 37 (*The Theory of Everything* film premiere, London, Britain – 09 Dec 2014), 40 (Stephen Hawking
and Elaine Mason/Manni Mason), Science Photo Library pp.13 (Stephen Hawking/Emilio Segre Visual Archives/
American Institute of Physics), 15 (Big Bang conceptual image/Deltev Van Ravensway), 16 (Conceptual image
of a clock spiralling into infinity/Robin Treadwell), 19 (Computer artwork of black hole/Mark Garlick),
20 (Professor Roger Penrose/Anthony Howarth), 43 (Stephen Hawking in freefall flight/NASA); Getty Images
pp.44 (Stephen Hawking's funeral/Christopher Furlong), Shutterstock pp.1 (Sydney Opera House/byvalet),
8 (punting on River Cam in Cambridge UK/Pajor Pawel), 10 (Night view of Trinity Hall College. Cambridge. UK/
Ilia Torlin), 21 (landmark entrance to the California Institute of Technology. Caltech/Ken Wolter), 53 (dinosaur
landscape/metha1819), 53 (ruins in Tunisia/Konstantin Aksenov), 53 (neandertals hunting bison/Nicolas
Primola); Prudence Upton p.2 (Stephen Hawking appearing by hologram technology at an event at Sydney
Opera House in 2015).

CONTENTS

1 Scientist and thinker

It was April 2015, and hundreds of people – young and old – were sitting in the famous Sydney Opera House in Australia. Great singers often come to the Opera House, but the people there that night did not come to listen to music. They paid a lot of money for tickets to hear a talk by a scientist – and there was not an empty seat in the room.

Everyone was excited when they saw the world-famous scientist who was going to speak. It was Stephen Hawking, but he was not really there. There was a hologram of him in the Opera House – a special picture of him that looked real! Stephen Hawking himself was thousands of kilometres away in Cambridge, England. He sat in his wheelchair. His body was still because he could only move his eyes and face, and he could only speak through a computer.

Sydney Opera House, Australia

Inside Sydney Opera House, 25th April 2015

'Hello, can you hear me?' he asked the crowd.

'Yes!' they shouted excitedly.

Stephen Hawking was one of the greatest thinkers of our time. That evening in Sydney, he talked about his life and his ideas, and he also told funny stories. At the end, when people left the Opera House, they talked about their wonderful evening. They also thought about some very big questions. Why are we here? Where did the universe come from? Does time have a beginning and an end? Stephen Hawking always tried to answer these questions, not just for scientists, but for ordinary listeners, too. Because he tried to explain things for people, and because of his great life story, he became a star.

Stephen Hawking had to use a wheelchair for most of his life — and he could not move, eat, or speak without help. So how did he live and work from day to day? When did he become famous? And what were his most important ideas?

2 Early years

Stephen William Hawking was born in Oxford, England, on 8th January 1942. On that same day, some people were remembering the death three hundred years earlier of another great man who studied the night sky, Galileo Galilei.

Stephen was the oldest of four children — he had two sisters and a much younger brother. His father Frank was a doctor and scientist who studied diseases. Stephen's father and his mother Isobel both had degrees from Oxford University, one of the best universities in the world. They were a very clever family, and the Hawkings often all sat and read books at the table while they were eating dinner. The family home during Stephen's earliest years was in Highgate, north London — Stephen was only born in Oxford because Britain was at war with Germany at that time, and people thought that London was too dangerous for babies.

Galileo Galilei

Young Stephen

A few years after the war, when Stephen was eight years old, the family moved to St Albans, a small town about 30 kilometres north of London. The Hawkings' house in St Albans was big, old, and very cold in winter, but Stephen loved it. He and his sister Mary liked to find lots of different ways into their house. They often climbed up the outside and then went in through open windows. Stephen was a good climber, and he sometimes climbed trees, too.

His mother Isobel often took her children out into the garden at night. On warm summer evenings, they lay on their backs and looked up at the night sky. Even then, Stephen was very interested in the stars. He also liked to ride bicycles, dance, and play tennis.

Stephen liked to understand how things worked, and he often built little aeroplanes and boats. Nobody had computers at home or school in those days, but when Stephen was sixteen, he and some school friends built a computer from pieces of old machines. It was not very good, but they could use it to do mathematics problems.

Stephen (far left) at St Albans School

Stephen did not like school very much, but he had some good friends there. They enjoyed talking together about things like science and music. Stephen's friends called him 'Einstein' because he was so clever. His teachers knew that he was clever, too, but he was always laughing and making jokes at school, and he did not work very hard. He was not a good student!

Stephen began to work harder in his last year at school because he wanted to study science at Oxford University. He became a student there, at University College, when he was only seventeen years old.

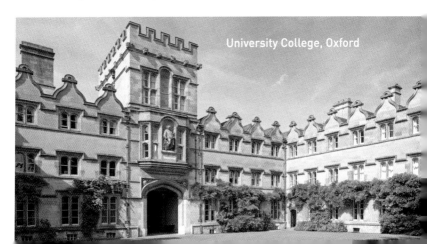
University College, Oxford

Stephen coxing, Oxford, 1961

He studied physics for his degree. Physics is very difficult to understand for most people, but it was easy for Stephen, so he did not have to work as hard as many other students. And Stephen did not need to write a lot of notes, because he could remember things very easily.

Stephen was younger than many of the other Oxford students, and he felt lonely at first, but that changed when he discovered rowing. Stephen was the cox: he did not row, but he sat at the front of the boat and told the rowers to go faster or slower, left or right. Stephen wanted his rowing team to go faster than the other teams, so he often did dangerous things to go past their boats. He sometimes took his team's boat very near to other boats, and even hit them!

After a difficult start, Stephen had a great time at Oxford. He had many friends in the rowing team, and he liked to listen to music with them and go to dances. Stephen often stayed out with his friends late at night, and had to climb over the walls to go back to his room because his college closed its doors at midnight.

Stephen leaving
Oxford University, 1962

Stephen left Oxford University in 1962 with a very good degree, so he decided to go to Cambridge University and study for a PhD. A PhD is a higher university degree, and anyone who wants to become an important scientist or teach at a university needs to get one.

The summer before he went to Cambridge, Stephen travelled across Europe with a friend, in trains and buses, and then went on to Iran. It was a wonderful journey, and for the first time, Stephen was far away from his family. He could go anywhere and do anything. He was a happy young man and he had a great life in front of him. But a few months later, everything changed.

3 Marriage

One day in Stephen's last year at Oxford University, he was walking down some stairs at his college when he suddenly fell. Friends helped him, but for a few minutes, Stephen could not remember who he was or anything about his life. The accident worried Stephen, but his doctor did not think that there was anything wrong with him. Nobody knew that he was really very ill.

Stephen started at Cambridge University in October 1962. He knew that he did not feel right, and his arms and legs were not as strong as before. But he tried to

Cambridge

forget about these problems and enjoy life. For his PhD, Stephen was studying cosmology: how the universe works. Cambridge was a good place for studying physics because it was home to many great scientists. It was a good place in other ways, too, because there were lots of young people, music, and parties.

Stephen went home to St Albans for the winter holidays in December 1962. There he saw his family and his old school friends, and he went to a New Year party. At the party, Stephen met a girl called Jane Wilde, and they soon became good friends.

Stephen was happy, and he looked well, too, but one day that winter, Stephen was outside with his mother when he fell, and could not get up. His mother took him to the doctor, and just after his birthday in January 1963,

Stephen went into hospital. The doctors kept him in hospital for two weeks, and at last, they explained what was wrong: Stephen had a disease called ALS. He was only twenty-one, and the doctors thought that he would only live for two more years.

Not many people get ALS, but it is a terrible disease. If you have ALS, it slowly becomes harder and harder to move your body. First, it becomes difficult to move your arms and legs, and then, after a time, you cannot eat, speak, or move your head. Usually, in the end, people with ALS die because they cannot breathe any more. When Stephen's mother asked a doctor, 'What can we do to fight the disease?', the answer was 'Nothing'.

This was a terrible time for Stephen, but he tried to be strong. One night, he had a strange dream. In the dream, some people wanted to kill him, and while he waited for death, Stephen thought about his life. Then he knew that he wanted to do lots of things. The dream helped Stephen. He knew now that he must not just feel sorry for himself. Perhaps he did not have a lot of time, but in that time, he needed to try and live an ordinary life. So, after some time at home, Stephen went back to Cambridge and began to study for his PhD again.

That June, Stephen took his friend Jane Wilde to a big summer party in his college, Trinity Hall. Music played and lights burned in the gardens of the beautiful five-hundred-year-old college. People laughed, ate, and talked.

Trinity Hall, Cambridge

Stephen could not move very well by then because his legs were not very strong any more. But Stephen and Jane listened to music, and they tried to dance. Stephen had blue-grey eyes and a big smile, and Jane liked being with him. Stephen liked Jane very much, too. She was clever, funny, and beautiful. For a few hours that evening, Stephen could try to forget about his troubles and enjoy life.

After that summer party, Stephen and Jane often met in London, because Jane was studying French and Spanish at university there. Jane knew that Stephen was very ill, but she loved him, and they decided to marry. This changed Stephen's life, and gave him hope for the future.

Jane and Stephen got married in July 1965. They did not have very much money, but they were happy together. Stephen now needed a stick to walk, and he could not easily hold a pen and write any more. But after two and a half years with ALS, he was still alive and doing well. Everything felt possible, and Stephen and Jane never talked about his disease — they both wanted to think about life, not death.

They went to America that summer. Stephen went to physics lectures at Cornell University, and he and Jane also visited many great places in New York. Did anyone see them when they stood at the top of the Empire State Building one day and looked down at the streets of Manhattan? When Stephen became a famous scientist, years later, everybody knew his name, but nobody knew him then. He was just another British visitor to New York: a young man standing next to his wife, on top of the world.

4   Theories and ideas

In 1964, the year before he got married, Stephen went to an important lecture in London by a British scientist called Fred Hoyle. At that time, Hoyle was one of the greatest scientists in Britain, and the room was full of famous and important people. Everyone listened carefully while Hoyle explained his latest theory in cosmology. But when it was time for questions, Stephen stood up and said that Hoyle was wrong.

Everybody looked at Stephen. He was only a young PhD student, and nobody knew who he was. But Stephen said that there was a mistake in the mathematics of Hoyle's theory. He said that it did not work. Of course, nobody in the room that day agreed with Stephen. But a few months after Hoyle's lecture, scientists found other problems with Hoyle's theory. Hoyle really was wrong.

Fred Hoyle

The Big Bang

Hoyle's theory of cosmology said that our universe has always been the same. But Stephen and some other cosmologists thought that the universe began suddenly a long time ago. The universe was very small at first, they said, but in seconds, it became much, much bigger – and it is still getting bigger today. People called this theory 'the Big Bang'. Today, cosmologists think that this is true, and they think that the Big Bang happened about 13.8 billion years ago. The Big Bang was one of the most important ideas in cosmology, and when Stephen was working on it, he was still only in his twenties.

Past   Present

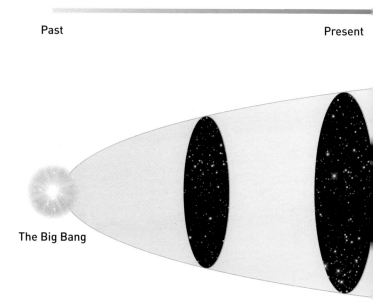

The Big Bang

The Big Bang

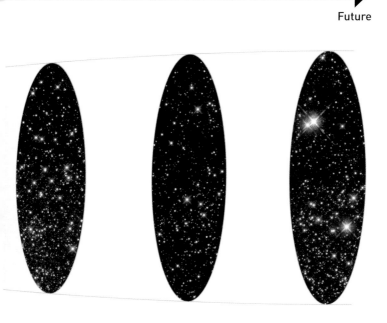

Future

Einstein and space-time

To understand Stephen's ideas, we first have to look at the theories of another great thinker – Albert Einstein. In 1905, Einstein had an important theory about space (the empty place between things) and time. Space is all around us: we can start in one place, walk around in space, and then go back to our starting place. But we cannot move around freely in time. Space and time feel different, but Einstein said that they are really two sides of the same thing – like two sides of a piece of paper. We call this 'space-time'.

Albert Einstein

Einstein also explained gravity. Gravity happens because things like stars 'push into' space-time and bend it. This is difficult to understand, but physics teachers explain the idea to their students like this: they take a big sheet of something which stretches (gets longer when you pull it). Then they ask two students to hold the sheet between them, and they put a heavy ball on it. The ball bends the sheet, just like a star bends space-time. When the teacher puts a lighter ball on the sheet, it moves closer to the big ball because the big ball is heavier and bends the sheet more. In the same way, because of gravity, lighter things always move closer to heavier things. For example, a small planet will always move closer to a big one.

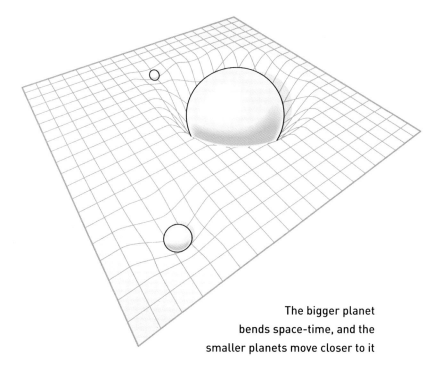

The bigger planet bends space-time, and the smaller planets move closer to it

Black holes

In Stephen's first years at Cambridge University, he used Einstein's theories to study one of the strangest things in the universe: black holes. When a star stops shining, gravity pulls everything in the dead star closer and closer together, and the star becomes smaller and smaller.

In the end, gravity pulls everything into one very, very small place in space. Because everything from the dead star is in one place, this bends space-time more and more, and at last, a hole is made. The gravity in this hole is very, very strong, so nothing can escape from it – not even light – and it becomes a 'black hole'. When things like other stars come too close to a black hole, they cannot escape its gravity. They fall into the black hole.

In the early 1960s, the scientist Roger Penrose discovered something new about black holes. He said that the centre of a black hole becomes smaller and smaller, and at last there is no space there. And because space and time are two sides of the same thing, time stops inside a black hole, too!

This gave Stephen his first great idea. In his PhD, he wrote about the universe at the time of the Big Bang. Stephen said that it was just like the centre of a black hole. Everything that later became the stars and planets was in one place: a place with no space and no time. Stephen said that you cannot ask 'Where did the Big Bang happen?' or 'What happened "before" the Big Bang?' These are questions about space and time – and there was no space or time before the Big Bang.

A black hole

5   A great cosmologist

After Stephen finished his PhD in March 1966, he went on working at Gonville and Caius College, Cambridge. Stephen's work in cosmology built on the theories of Roger Penrose, and in the 1960s and 1970s, Stephen studied black holes with him and others. Together, they discovered a lot of important things about the universe – for example, how black holes begin and what happens inside them. They also asked questions about what happens when two black holes meet.

Roger Penrose

Hawking and Penrose won a lot of prizes for their work, too, like the Gravity Foundation Prize and the Adams Prize. Stephen became the world's number one black hole scientist. His work was very important, because when cosmologists know about black holes, they can understand many other things about the universe, for example, how it began and what will happen to it in the end.

Stephen was teaching at Cambridge University at this time, but in 1974, there was a big change for him. An important university in California called California Institute of Technology (Caltech) asked Stephen to teach there for a year – so the family went to live in the USA. Stephen and Jane made lots of friends there. Their house was very close to the university, and it was always full of scientists and other friends at the weekends. They had parties and dinners, and Stephen often sat with his friends and talked about science late into the night.

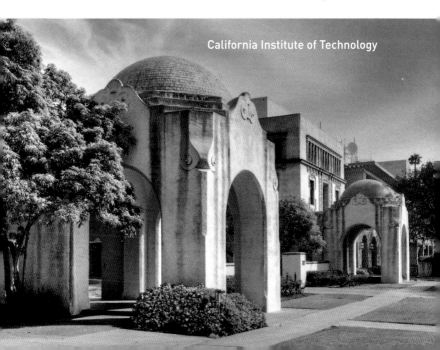

California Institute of Technology

At Caltech, Stephen worked with some of the greatest names in physics and cosmology. In 1974, Stephen gave an important lecture, and he explained something very surprising. Nothing escapes from *inside* a black hole, he said, but radiation comes from a place *around* the black hole. Because radiation is escaping from around the black hole, the black hole slowly becomes smaller and smaller – and after a long time, there is no black hole any more. Many cosmologists just laughed at this idea when Stephen first explained it, but most people today think that it is true.

Soon after this, while Stephen was still in California, he had some important news. A letter arrived which asked him to be one of the scientists in London's world-famous Royal Society. This was a great and exciting thing for a thirty-two-year-old scientist.

The Hawkings went back to Britain in 1975, and Stephen started work at Cambridge University again. He was doing very important work in cosmology at this time, and by the end of the 1970s, physicists everywhere knew about him. He was also getting prizes and special degrees from universities and societies around the world.

Stephen in 1979

Then, in 1979, Stephen became Cambridge University's Lucasian Professor of Mathematics. This job is for the very best mathematicians and physicists, and some of the greatest names in science have been Lucasian Professor in the past. One Lucasian Professor was Isaac Newton, the father of modern physics and the man who discovered gravity in the late 1600s. Now Stephen was one of these great people, too.

Stephen's work brought together many different ideas in physics for the first time, and this started him on a new journey. He wanted to find a 'theory of everything' – one theory that we can use to understand any question in physics, like 'How did the universe begin?' and 'What is everything really made of?' No one has found a theory of everything yet, but many scientists are working on the problem. One day, perhaps, if they find this theory, we can use it to build wonderful new machines, or even travel to the stars! It only became possible for people to visit the moon because of past theories in physics – that is how important these theories are.

Isaac Newton

Stephen in 1988

Some of Stephen's theories about the universe changed a lot over the years, and sometimes Stephen was wrong about things, too. But this is not unusual in science – even the great Albert Einstein made some mistakes. Stephen was not afraid to ask big questions, for example, 'Will people travel in time one day?', 'Can scientists make small black holes here on Earth?', and 'Are there other universes?' We do not know the answers to these questions, but thanks to Stephen, we are beginning to understand how to study them.

6　A new voice

In 1963, doctors said that Stephen would only live for about two more years. But fifteen years later, he was still alive. His disabilities became a little worse every year, and he had many problems, but he did not stop working — and he never lost hope.

After 1969, Stephen had to use a wheelchair. He could not use his hands very much by then, so Jane had to write the words for Stephen's lectures for him — and she also had to look after him. By the late 1970s, Stephen could not use a lot of his body. His arms were not strong any more, and he could not speak easily. Only Stephen's family and close friends could understand his voice, so when he gave a lecture, a scientist friend or a student always helped him. He spoke quietly to them, and then they said his words to everyone in the room.

By this time, Stephen could not write notes, so he had to remember everything. He was already good at this, but now he had to be really good. He found special ways to remember things, and he learned to read something once or listen to a lecture once, and then keep it all in his head.

Physicists write lots of difficult mathematics when they think about problems, but Stephen could not write, so he had to work in a different way. When Stephen thought about a problem in physics, he usually used pictures in his head, and not mathematics, to find the answers.

And because Stephen thought about things in a different way, he had different and new ideas. He did not have to look at lots of books or sit at a desk when he was working. He carried all his ideas about a new theory in his head, so he could think about it at any time. Once, he discovered something important about black holes when he was getting into bed!

In 1985, Stephen was meeting with other scientists in Switzerland when he became very ill. He could not breathe without a machine, and the doctors thought that he would die. They wanted to turn off the machine, but Stephen's wife Jane stopped them doing this. For weeks, Stephen was very near to death. Friends and family stayed by his bed − they talked to him, read books to him, and hoped for him. And he lived.

When Stephen was a little stronger, doctors in England opened a hole in his throat. Now he could breathe through the hole, and without a machine. But Stephen needed the help of nurses twenty-four hours a day − and he could not speak any more.

Stephen now needed to talk to people and ask for things in a different way. At first, he used a special A–Z to 'talk'. Friends and nurses held up the letters A–Z, and Stephen moved his eyes when someone showed him the right letter. In this way, his helper could write his words. But talking like this was very difficult and slow.

Stephen wanted something better, so his friends spoke

Stephen using his
special machine

to somebody who made computers and machines for people with disabilities. After a lot of hard work, a special machine was made just for Stephen. With this machine, Stephen had to look at lots of words on a computer, and then touch a little box in his hand for the right word. In this way, Stephen could write about fifteen words a minute.

By the end of 1985, Stephen's machine had a special 'voice': when he wrote on the computer, the 'voice' spoke slowly for him. Stephen's new computer voice sounded strange – like a robot – but it helped him a lot. Before, when he spoke, most people could not understand what he was saying. Now, suddenly, he could talk to anybody again – even a big room full of people – as loud as he wanted.

Stephen's computer changed over the years because his disease became worse – and computers became better. In the end, he had to wear a small camera because he could not use either of his hands any more. When he found a word on the computer, he moved his face a little. The camera saw this and wrote the word. Stephen could only find three words in a minute, so it took him hours to write or say anything. Writing on a voice computer is very difficult, but Stephen wrote many important lectures – and seven books – like this!

camera

Stephen's computer voice did not change after 1985. There were lots of new and better computer voices, but Stephen did not want a new one. His voice became as famous as him, and when Stephen spoke, everyone knew who it was!

Stephen used a small camera and a computer to speak

7   A big name

A CBE

By the middle of the 1970s, cosmologists everywhere knew about Stephen because of his work on black holes. Ordinary people in Britain began to hear his name more after he was on British TV in *Professor Hawking's Universe* in the 1980s. Stephen also got an important British award called a CBE in 1982. After he got that award, he was often on TV and in the newspapers – first in Britain, and then around the world.

Of course, for many people, the story of Stephen's life was as interesting as his ideas about physics. He was so clever, but he had a body with terrible disabilities. He could understand the universe, but he could not move his arms or legs. And after twenty years with a deadly disease, he was still alive! Stephen Hawking's story was wonderful, but people also loved him as a person. He could explain difficult ideas in science, and when he talked about them, they became interesting. He always had a funny, clever reply for every question, too.

Explaining science on TV gave Stephen a great idea. He decided to write a book about cosmology for ordinary people, not scientists. Many people said that it was not possible. They did not think that anyone would want to read a book like that. But Stephen did not listen.

When Stephen began to work on his book, *A Brief History of Time*, in 1982, he spoke the words to someone who wrote them for him. But after he lost his voice in 1985, he had to finish the book on his voice computer, writing very, very slowly. Stephen also needed to change some pages of the book again and again — because he wanted ordinary people to understand it easily.

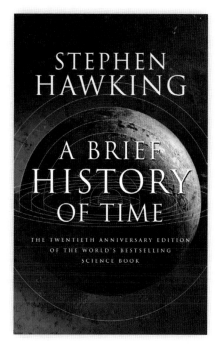

At last, in 1988, after a lot of very hard work, the book was ready. And when it began selling in the shops later that year, people loved it.

More than ten million people bought *A Brief History of Time*, and you can now read it in forty different languages. Stephen travelled a lot to talk about the book, and in many towns around the world, people waited for hours to see him. Stephen got lots of letters and emails about *A Brief History of Time*. Readers wrote to him and said how much they enjoyed it.

So why did people like *A Brief History of Time* so much? Perhaps because it asked many important questions, and because people who read it understood for the first time how wonderful our universe really is.

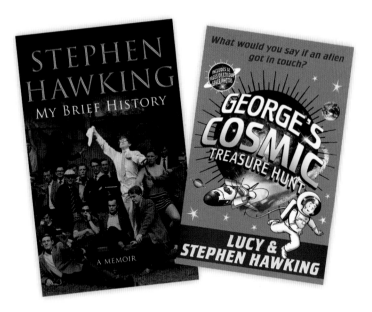

Many young people became interested in science – and perhaps became scientists – because of Stephen's book.

After *A Brief History of Time*, Stephen wrote more science books for ordinary readers, and a book about his life, called *My Brief History*.

Stephen wanted children to understand science and cosmology, too, so he wrote some books for children with his daughter, the writer Lucy Hawking. In the books, a young boy called George travels around the universe with his friends. He visits places like black holes and does some wonderful things. The books are great stories, but they are also science books. They explain physics and cosmology in an easy way for children.

Stephen Hawking's theories, books, and life story made him one of the most famous people on Earth. People from newspapers and the TV were always asking to talk to him, and his office in Cambridge was often full of cameras. People did not just want to know what Stephen thought about cosmology. They asked him for his ideas about anything – from computers to football and pop music. Stephen liked to make jokes, too, and he was on TV in *The Simpsons* and *The Big Bang Theory*. There are also two great films about his life.

It was not always easy to be famous. But because everyone knew Stephen's name, he could do many things that were important to him – speaking against wars and helping children with disabilities, for example.

Stephen in *The Big Bang Theory*, 2012

With Barack Obama, 2009

Stephen and Jane worked hard to help people with ALS. Jane visited people with the disease in their homes, and Stephen and Jane did many things to get money for ALS charities. Being famous helped their work. Before Stephen became ill, not many people knew about ALS, but now, a lot of people have heard about it. Today, ALS charities are working to try to stop this terrible disease, and people have given millions of pounds to help them.

In the 1980s and 1990s, Stephen travelled all over the world to give lectures and meet with scientists. When he travelled, he also often met with groups of children who had disabilities. He answered their questions, told them stories from his life, and gave them hope. He worked with a charity called SOS Children's Villages, too. The charity helps children who have no mothers and fathers, and tries to give them a better future.

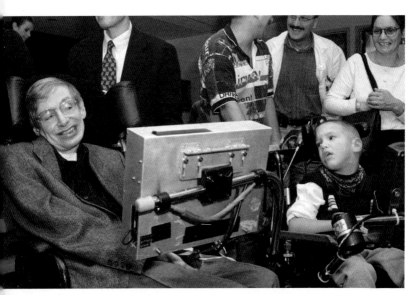

Stephen visiting a children's hospital, Boston, 1999

On 29th August 2012, Stephen spoke at the opening of the London Paralympic Games. More than sixty-two thousand people were there that night, and millions more were watching on TV around the world. At the opening, Stephen talked about how nobody is ordinary – everyone is different. And he said that everyone can be good at something – even people who have very difficult lives. Stephen showed this, and there are not many people in the world, with or without disabilities, who are as important or as famous as he was.

Stephen at the London Paralympic Games, 2012

8　Family life

In December 2014, Stephen and Jane Hawking went to London for the first night of a new film about their lives, *The Theory of Everything*. The film was made from a book by Jane. Felicity Jones played Jane, and Eddie Redmayne played Stephen – and he won an Oscar and many other awards for it.

Eddie Redmayne and Felicity Jones in *The Theory of Everything*

Stephen and Jane with Eddie Redmayne and Felicity Jones

Stephen and Jane smiled for photos with the stars of the film, and they looked very happy when they went down the red carpet and into the cinema. But life was never easy for them, and *The Theory of Everything* showed people that.

When Jane married Stephen, she knew that he had ALS. They both thought that Stephen would not live very long, but they wanted to be together and have a family. In 1967, Stephen and Jane's first child, Robert, was born, and a few years later, they had a daughter called Lucy. Stephen could not do many ordinary things with the children – he could not take them to school or play with them in the garden. But he tried to be a good father, and he loved being with his children.

Stephen and Jane's third child, Tim, was born in 1979. He was much younger than the other Hawking children and, by this time, Stephen was already using a wheelchair and he could not speak very much. For the first years of Tim's life, he could not really understand his father's voice. He and his father could only have a real conversation after Stephen got his voice computer. But Tim and Stephen spent a lot of time together. Like his father, Tim enjoyed making jokes – and he liked driving his father's wheelchair around the house!

At that time, it was not easy to live in a place like Cambridge if you had to use a wheelchair. When Jane and Stephen went out, they had problems with holes in the roads, places that had no space for a wheelchair, and buildings with lots of stairs. They often had to ask for help when they wanted to go into a shop or just cross the street. So they decided to fight for the needs of people with disabilities, and they wrote letters to newspapers and to important people.

They also went out in the streets with other people who had disabilities, and their families, and called for change. All around Britain, groups of people with disabilities talked about how difficult life was for them. And slowly, more people began to listen to their needs. Roads and buildings all around Britain began to change, and at last, people with disabilities could use them more easily.

Stephen needed a lot of help all day and night, and he often had to go into hospital. For many years, Jane was studying for a PhD, but she also had to look after the children, wash and dress Stephen, tidy the house, cook,

Stephen and Jane

and give Stephen his food one piece at a time. And when it was time for bed, Jane and another helper had to carry Stephen up the stairs.

When Stephen, Jane, and the children were in America in 1974, a PhD student lived with the family and helped at home. Stephen and Jane thought that this was a good idea – so back in Britain, for many years, different PhD students lived with them in their house in Cambridge, and looked after Stephen with Jane. Nurses and other people visited them all the time, too, so the house was always full of people. It was not easy for the Hawkings to be alone, and they could not have an ordinary family life.

Stephen marrying Elaine Mason, 1995

Stephen and Jane's marriage came to an end in 1990. In 1995, Stephen married his nurse, Elaine Mason, and they were together for eleven years. After that, he lived alone, but people visited his house and looked after him twenty-four hours a day. Jane married again in 1997, but she was always good friends with Stephen. They often met and saw their children and grandchildren together.

Lucy and Tim Hawking went with their mother and father to the first night of the film *The Theory of Everything*. They watched when Eddie Redmayne danced with Felicity Jones – the woman in the film who played their mother. They watched when a young 'Stephen Hawking' rode a bicycle, went out in a boat, and enjoyed himself with friends. And when Tim sat there in the dark cinema, he cried a little – because he never saw his father do those things in real life.

9   Last years

In February 2016, some cosmologists discovered what happens when two black holes meet. Stephen was not one of these scientists, but people wanted to know what he thought about the news. 'What does it mean?' they asked. 'How important is this?' Stephen explained the cosmologists' work, and why it was important, in a way that ordinary people could understand. People around the world were always interested in Stephen's ideas. We listened to Stephen Hawking because he was one of the greatest thinkers of our time.

When Stephen began his work on black holes, many people asked, 'Are black holes real or not?' But today, scientists think that there are black holes everywhere in space. There is even a black hole in the centre of our galaxy, and it is bigger than a million suns! Are Stephen's other theories right, too? We still do not know, and we will not know for many years.

Cosmologists know that we live on an ordinary planet near an ordinary star in an ordinary galaxy. They say that our galaxy is one of billions out there in space. Perhaps life is 'ordinary', too, but Stephen thought that *people* are not ordinary, because we have science. Because of science, we have learned how to look at the world around us and ask questions. We have begun to understand what the universe is, how it began, and why we are here. And because of this, Stephen thought that we are very special.

Science has changed the lives of everyone on Earth, and Stephen thought that it is very important for our future. But science can also bring dangers, he said. We are building robots that are better and better all the time, and Stephen thought that perhaps one day, somebody will use robot soldiers which can kill millions of people in a war. Scientists are also trying to make computers which can think. But when we build them, will these computers become cleverer than us? We must be careful and learn how to use these computers, Stephen thought – before they learn how to use us!

But Stephen had a lot of hope for the future, too. He thought that one day, people will build wonderful new machines and travel through the galaxy. They will

Our galaxy

discover new worlds, and will perhaps decide to live far away from Earth.

Stephen always wanted to go into space himself. He never did this, but in 2007, he flew in a special plane from the Kennedy Space Center in the USA. The plane climbed high into the sky above Florida, then suddenly came down very fast. The people inside were falling to Earth, but the plane was flying down just as fast – so the passengers felt no gravity for about twenty-five seconds. It was like being in space! Stephen loved the feeling of 'zero gravity'. He smiled from ear to ear while helpers turned his body around and around.

Stephen in 'zero gravity'

Stephen died on 14th March 2018 – he was born on the day when Galileo Galilei died, and he died on the day when another great thinker, Albert Einstein, was born. Only two weeks before his death, Stephen finished his last important scientific work. In it, he wrote about the end of our universe, and how we will perhaps find other universes one day, too.

For many years, Stephen could not move his body or speak. Life was very difficult for him, but he never stopped working, thinking, and asking big, important questions. He was one of the greatest scientists of his time. But more importantly, perhaps, he helped non-scientists to understand physics, cosmology, and the world around us. Stephen Hawking opened our eyes to the universe – and because of him, we know how wonderful it is to be here.

Stephen Hawking's funeral

award *(n)* a prize or money that you give to somebody who has done something very well

bang *(n)* a sudden very loud noise

become *(v)* to begin to be something

bend *(v)* to change the shape of something, e.g. if you push it or put something heavy on it

breathe *(v)* to take air in and out through your nose and mouth

brief *(adj)* short or quick

charity *(n)* an organization of people who work together to get money and give it to other people who need help

close *(adj)* near

college *(n)* a place in a university where you live and study after you have left school

degree *(n)* what a university or college gives you at the end of your study time there

disability *(n)* when you cannot use a part of your body well or easily, or cannot learn easily

discover *(v)* to find or learn something for the first time

disease *(n)* When someone has a disease, they become ill.

dream *(n)* a picture in your head when you are sleeping

Earth *(n)* this world; the planet that we live on

future *(n)* time that will come, e.g. tomorrow

galaxy *(n)* a very large group of stars

grandchild *(n)* the child of your son or daughter

gravity *(n)* Gravity pulls things and holds them together, e.g. apples fall from trees because gravity pulls the apples.

history *(n)* all the things that happened before now

idea *(n)* a plan, or something you think of

joke *(n)* something funny that you say or do

lecture *(n)* when somebody talks to a group of people and teaches them about something; a lesson at a university

light *(adj)* not heavy

look after *(v)* to help a person or animal, and do things for them

machine *(n)* a thing which is made to do a job

marriage *(n)* to be husband and wife

mathematics *(n)*   learning about numbers; **mathematician** *(n)*

ordinary *(adj)*   not special or unusual

planet *(n)*   something large and round in space that moves around the sun or another star

prize *(n)*   what people give to somebody who has done something very well, or who wins something

problem *(n)*   something that is difficult; something that you worry about; a question, e.g. in mathematics

professor *(n)*   a teacher at a college or university

radiation *(n)*   energy from hot things like the sun, that goes out into space

robot *(n)*   a machine that can work like a person

row *(v)*   to move a boat in the water with long sticks called oars; **rowing** *(n)*

science *(n)* learning about our world; **scientist** *(n)*

sheet *(n)*   a thin piece of something, e.g. paper or glass

space *(n)*   the empty place between things; the place outside Earth, where all the other planets and stars are

study *(v)*   to learn about something

team *(n)*   a group of people who do something together against another group

theory *(n)*   an idea that tries to explain something

throat *(n)*   a place inside your neck where food goes down from your mouth into your body

universe *(n)*   the Earth and all the stars, planets, and everything in space

university *(n)*   Many young people go to a university to study after they have left college.

war *(n)*   fighting between countries or between groups of people

wheelchair *(n)*   a chair with wheels for people who cannot walk easily

The life of Stephen Hawking

1942	• Born in Oxford on 8th January.
1950	• The family go to live in St Albans.
1959	• Goes to Oxford University to study physics.
1962	• Begins to study cosmology at Cambridge University. • Meets Jane Wilde.
1963	• Doctors know that Stephen has a disease that is called ALS.
1965	• Marries Jane Wilde.
1966	• Finishes his PhD about 'the Big Bang'.
1967	• His first child, Robert, is born.
1970	• His daughter, Lucy, is born.
1974	• Starts to teach at Caltech. In an important lecture, he explains that radiation can come from around black holes.
1975	• Goes back to Britain and starts teaching at Cambridge University.
1979	• Becomes Lucasian Professor of Mathematics at Cambridge University. • His third child, Tim, is born.
1982	• Gets an important award – the CBE. • Starts his first book, *A Brief History of Time*.
1985	• Has a serious illness. Loses his voice and starts to speak through a computer.
1988	• Finishes *A Brief History of Time*, and people start to buy it.
1990	• His marriage to Jane ends.
1995	• Marries Elaine Mason.
2007	• Flies in zero gravity.
2012	• Speaks at the opening of the London Paralympic Games.
2014	• Goes to the film about his life, *The Theory of Everything*.
2018	• Dies in Cambridge on 14th March.

Lucasian Professors of Mathematics

Stephen Hawking was the Lucasian Professor of Mathematics at Cambridge University between 1979 and 2009. Here are some other scientists who have had this job.

Isaac Newton
Lucasian Professor 1669–1702
Isaac Newton discovered new things about gravity. He also discovered many things about light, and how things move. His ideas are important for all physicists.

Charles Babbage
Lucasian Professor 1828–1839
Charles Babbage studied mathematics, and he built a machine that could do mathematics many years before the first computers were made.

Paul Dirac
Lucasian Professor 1932–1969
Paul Dirac had many big ideas about physics, and he won the Nobel Prize in Physics in 1933. His work helped other physicists. Dirac's ideas are still important, and people have used them, for example, to make machines for hospitals.

Three important sciences

Physics

Physics is the study of how everything around us works, and what it is made of. For example, physicists study how things move, how gravity works, and what light is.

Astronomy

Astronomy is the study of things like planets, stars, and galaxies. Astronomers often use telescopes to see far into space. Because of their work, it is easier for us to understand things in space, and learn how the universe is changing.

Cosmology

Cosmology uses physics and astronomy. Cosmologists think about and try to answer important questions about the universe. For example, how did the universe begin, why is it becoming bigger, and what will happen in the future?

A brief history of the universe

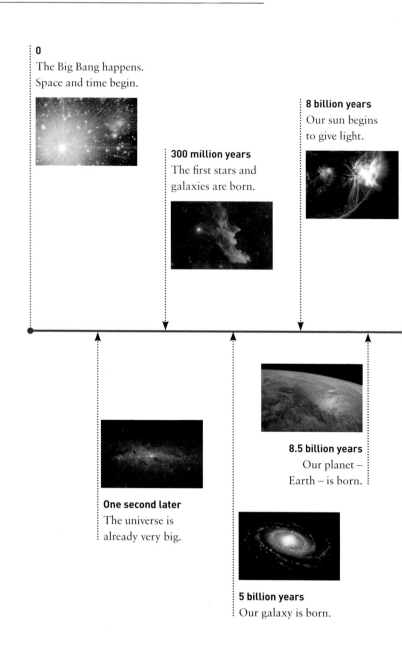

0
The Big Bang happens.
Space and time begin.

300 million years
The first stars and
galaxies are born.

8 billion years
Our sun begins
to give light.

One second later
The universe is
already very big.

8.5 billion years
Our planet –
Earth – is born.

5 billion years
Our galaxy is born.

230 million years ago
The first dinosaurs
live on Earth.

Today
Scientists like Stephen Hawking
try to understand the Big Bang
and the universe.

9,000 years ago
The first towns are built.

400 years ago
Galileo Galilei
studies the night sky.

200,000 years ago
The first people walk on Earth.

Stephen Hawking

ACTIVITIES

Think ahead

1 **Read the back cover. What are you going to read about in this book? Tick (✓) six things.**

space ☐   being famous ☐   a book ☐
family ☐   disabilities ☐   cooking ☐
clothes ☐   a computer ☐   singing ☐

2 **What do you know about Stephen Hawking? Choose the correct words to complete the sentences.**

1 Stephen Hawking was a famous *scientist / cook*.

2 He wrote many books about *cars / space*.

3 His first wife's name was *Jane / Elaine*.

4 He *had / didn't have* an easy life.

5 He *spoke / listened* through a computer.

3 **RESEARCH Find out the answers to these questions about Stephen Hawking.**

1 Where did Stephen Hawking live for most of his life?

2 What is the name of the film about his life which was made in 2014?

Chapter check

CHAPTER 1 Are these sentences true or false?

1 When Stephen Hawking spoke at the Sydney Opera House, it was nearly empty.
2 The tickets were free.
3 Stephen was not really in Sydney that night.
4 Stephen only spoke about science.
5 Stephen told some funny stories.
6 Stephen could explain important ideas about the universe to people.

CHAPTER 2 Put the sentences in the correct order, 1–6.

a Stephen discovered rowing.
b Stephen arrived at Cambridge University.
c Stephen travelled to Iran with a friend.
d Stephen began to study science at Oxford University.
e Stephen and some friends built a computer.
f Stephen's family moved to St Albans.

CHAPTER 3 Correct the <u>underlined</u> words.

1 Stephen was <u>sad</u> after he had an accident.
2 Doctors knew what was wrong: Stephen had a <u>theory</u> called ALS.
3 People with ALS can't <u>feel</u> their bodies easily.
4 One night, Stephen had a strange <u>idea</u>, and then he went back to Cambridge University.
5 Stephen and Jane went to a <u>lecture</u> at Trinity Hall.
6 By the summer of 1965, Stephen could not walk or <u>talk</u> easily.

CHAPTER 4 Complete the sentences with the correct words.

scientist   stars   theories   time   universe

1 Stephen said that one of Hoyle's _____ was
   wrong.
2 Stephen and some other cosmologists thought that the
   _____ started suddenly and became big very
   quickly.
3 Einstein was a _____ who had important ideas.
4 If _____ come too close to a black hole, they fall
   into it.
5 Stephen thought that there was no _____ or
   space before the Big Bang.

CHAPTER 5 Tick (✓) the three sentences which are true.

1 Stephen left Cambridge after he finished his PhD.
2 Stephen worked with Roger Penrose, and they got prizes
   together.
3 Stephen and Jane went to live in the USA.
4 In 1974, Stephen gave an important lecture about
   black holes.
5 In the 1970s, scientists didn't know who Stephen was.

CHAPTER 6 Match the sentence halves.

1 Stephen's disabilities became worse each year, but...
2 After 1969, Stephen had to use...
3 In 1985, Stephen became very ill, and...
4 Stephen could not speak any more, so he used...

a a wheelchair.
b doctors thought that he would die.
c a special computer with a voice.
d he never lost hope.

CHAPTER 7 Choose the correct answers.

1 Stephen began to write *A Brief History of Time* in ... .
   a 1970   b 1982   c 1988
2 Stephen wanted ... people to understand the universe.
   a clever   b important   c ordinary
3 More than ... million people have bought *A Brief History of Time*.
   a one   b four   c ten
4 Stephen and his daughter Lucy wrote books about the universe for ... .
   a scientists   b children   c doctors
5 People want to know ... of Stephen's ideas.
   a all   b some   c none
6 Stephen spoke at the opening of the Paralympic Games in ... .
   a 2008   b 2012   c 2016

CHAPTER 8 Choose the correct words to complete the sentences.

1 Stephen and Jane's life was never *happy / easy*.

2 Stephen could not *spend time / play* with his children.

3 Stephen was already using a *voice computer / wheelchair* when Tim was born.

4 When Stephen and his family were in America, a *nurse / student* lived with them, and helped at home.

5 Jane was still Stephen's *friend / wife* after 1990.

CHAPTER 9 Complete the sentences with the correct words.

black holes   future   galaxy   gravity   science   worlds

1 Today, people know that _____ are real.

2 Our _____ is one of billions in space.

3 Stephen thought that people are special because we have _____.

4 Stephen had a lot of hope for the _____.

5 Stephen thought that people will find new _____ one day, and perhaps live far away from Earth.

6 When Stephen flew in a special plane, he felt no _____ for a short time.

Focus on vocabulary

1 Write the words.

1 teams of people do this sport in boats
2 a picture in your head when you are sleeping
3 something large and round in space, like Earth
4 a group of millions of stars
5 something you get if you win or have done something very well
6 a chair with wheels for people who cannot walk easily
7 to learn about something

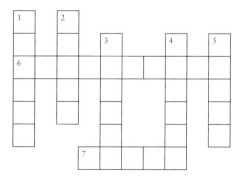

2 Replace the <u>underlined</u> words with the words below.

discovered   lecture   professor   space

1 Einstein knew a lot about <u>the empty place between things</u> and time.
2 In 1964, Stephen went to hear a <u>talk</u> by Fred Hoyle.
3 Stephen <u>learned</u> many things about the universe.
4 In 1979, Stephen became a <u>very important teacher</u>.

Focus on language

1 **Complete the sentences using *to* and the correct words.**

explain science to children   find answers
help people with ALS   speak to people

1 Physicists use difficult mathematics _____.
2 Stephen used a computer voice _____.
3 Stephen and Lucy wrote books _____.
4 People have given a lot of money to charities
_____.

2 **DECODE** **Read the text from the story, and <u>underline</u> *when*
and *because*. Then tick (✓) the correct sentences.**

When a star stops shining, gravity pulls everything in the
dead star closer and closer together, and the star becomes
smaller and smaller. In the end, gravity pulls everything
into one very, very small place in space. Because everything
from the dead star is in one place, this bends space-time
more and more, and at last, a hole is made.

1 a ☐ Old stars shine after black holes happen.
  b ☐ Old stars stop shining and then there are
       black holes.
2 a ☐ Gravity bends space-time and makes a hole.
  b ☐ The dead star pulls gravity and bends space-time.

Discussion

1 Read the dialogue. What do the speakers agree and
   disagree about?

   A: Science is so interesting. I want to know about space
      and the universe.
   B: You never will! Ordinary people can't understand
      cosmology. It's too difficult.
   A: But Stephen Hawking wrote a book about space for
      ordinary people. He thought that we can understand it.
   B: Well, I disagree. And, in my opinion, scientists don't
      know very much. No one can know about space.
   A: Perhaps you're right. But I still think that it's interesting.

2 Complete the phrases from the conversation in exercise 1
   for giving your opinion, agreeing, or disagreeing. Write O,
   A, or D.

   1 In my _____, ...   3 Perhaps _____ ...
   2 Well, I _____ ...   4 I still _____ that ...

3 **THINK CRITICALLY** Discuss the statements below with a
   partner. Use the phrases in exercise 2.

   1 Stephen had many problems, but he had a good life.
   2 The future will be better than the present for most
      people on Earth.

1 **Match the famous scientists to the things they studied or discovered.**

1	Marie Curie	a	$E=mc^2$
2	Albert Einstein	b	electricity
3	Alessandro Volta	c	evolution
4	Charles Darwin	d	DNA
5	Rosalind Franklin	e	radiation

2 **Now read the story about the scientist Galileo Galilei. Why did he have to stay at home at the end of his life?**

Galileo Galilei was born in Pisa (now in Italy) on 15th February 1564. He was the oldest of six children. His father wrote and played music, and Galileo became very good at music, too. Galileo became interested in science while he was studying at Pisa University. He wanted to be a doctor. He later wrote about and taught mathematics, physics, and astronomy. Galileo studied physics: he learned how and why things move, and what they are made of. He also studied the night sky, and he discovered moons around the planet Jupiter.

Galileo said that the Earth moved around the sun, but this was a new idea. And some important people in the church did not agree with him. They said that the sun moved around the Earth. In 1633, they told Galileo not to speak about his idea. They did not want him to write about science or leave his house again. So Galileo lived at his house near Florence until he died in 1642. But he secretly studied science, and did not stop thinking and writing. Because of Galileo's work, we can understand our world better. Today, people call Galileo the father of modern science because he tested his theories, like modern scientists.

3 Choose one of the scientists in exercise 1. Write three questions about their life and their work.

4 **CREATE** Now find out more information about your scientist and answer your questions from exercise 3.

5 **COLLABORATE** In small groups, describe your scientist to your friends. Then, as a group, decide which scientist is the most important, and why.

If you liked this Bookworm, why not try...

John F. Kennedy

STAGE 2
Anne Collins

'Ask not what your country can do for you –
ask what you can do for your country.'
More than fifty years ago, the new US
president, John F. Kennedy, spoke these
words. Millions of Americans listened. With
Kennedy as president, Americans were
filled with hope. But in November 1963, the world stopped as
terrible news came...

Leonardo da Vinci

STAGE 2
Alex Raynham

'What does the world look like from the
moon?' 'How do our bodies work?' 'Is it
possible for people to fly?' 'Can I make a
horse of bronze eight metres tall?' 'How
can we have cleaner cities?' All his life,
Leonardo da Vinci asked questions. We
know him as a great artist, but he was also one of the great
thinkers of all time. Even today, doctors and scientists are still
learning from his ideas. Meet the man who made a robot lion,
wrote backwards, and tried to win a war by moving a river.